I0056761

THE COMPLETE FINOPS HANDBOOK

ESSENTIAL TOOLS AND TECHNIQUES FOR FINANCIAL OPERATIONS

PETER BATES

Book
Bound Studios

Copyright © 2022 by Peter Bates

All rights reserved. No part of this book may be reproduced, stored in a retrieval system, or transmitted in any form or by any means, electronic, mechanical, photocopying, recording, or otherwise, without the prior written permission of the publisher, Book Bound Studios.

The information contained in this book is based on the author's personal experiences and research. While every effort has been made to ensure the accuracy of the information presented, the author and publisher cannot be held responsible for any errors or omissions. The information in this book is not intended as medical or legal advice, and should not be used as such.

This book is intended for general informational purposes only and is not a substitute for professional medical or legal advice. If you have specific questions about any medical or legal matters, you should consult with a qualified healthcare professional or attorney.

Book Bound Studios is not affiliated with any product or vendor mentioned in this book. The views expressed in this book are those of the author and do not necessarily reflect the views of Book Bound Studios.

To all the FinOps professionals and aspiring professionals out there,

I dedicate this book to you and your dedication to managing financial operations effectively and efficiently. Your hard work and dedication to the field of FinOps are what inspire me to share my knowledge and experience with you.

May this book serve as a helpful guide and resource as you navigate your career in financial operations and strive to achieve your goals and objectives. I appreciate your commitment to excellence in this important and ever-evolving field.

Sincerely, Peter Bates

"The art of good business is being a good middleman."

MALCOLM GLADWELL, "THE TIPPING POINT"

CONTENTS

Foreword   ix

Introduction to FinOps   xi

1. Budgeting and Forecasting in FinOps   1
   Essential Tools for Planning and Managing Financial Resources

2. Financial Reporting in FinOps   7
   Understanding and Analyzing Key Financial Documents

3. Cost Management in FinOps   11
   Identifying and Eliminating Waste to Increase Efficiency and Profitability

4. Financial Analysis in FinOps   15
   Evaluating and Improving Financial Performance through Ratio Analysis and Trend Analysis

5. Financial Modeling in FinOps   19
   Simulating Different Scenarios to Inform Future Financial Strategies

6. Risk Management in FinOps   23
   Protecting Financial Assets through Insurance and Hedging

7. Treasury Management in FinOps   27
   Managing Cash Flow, Debt, and Surplus Funds

8. Compliance in FinOps   31
   Ensuring Adherence to Financial Regulations and Laws

Using FinOps to Drive Success   35
   A Case Study

The Importance of FinOps in Financial Management and Operations   39

Afterword   41

Acknowledgments   43

About the Author   45

FOREWORD

As someone who has spent many years working in financial operations, I am *thrilled* to see a comprehensive guide to FinOps being published. The tools and techniques of FinOps are essential for managing financial resources effectively and making informed decisions. This book does an excellent job of covering all of the key topics and activities for which professionals in this field are responsible.

Whether you are a beginner looking to get a foothold in the field or an experienced professional seeking to expand your knowledge, this book has something to offer you. The clear explanations and practical examples make the concepts easy to understand and apply, and the tips and best practices provide valuable insights into overcoming the challenges and pitfalls of FinOps.

I highly recommend this book to anyone interested in advancing their career in financial operations or learning more about this exciting and rewarding field. With its comprehensive coverage and practical approach, it is sure to become an invaluable resource for professionals at all levels.

Sincerely, Peter Bates

INTRODUCTION TO FINOPS
AN OVERVIEW OF FINANCIAL OPERATIONS

Financial operations, or *FinOps*, play a crucial role in any organization's financial management and operations. As a FinOps professional, you are responsible for a wide range of activities that help to inform decision-making, strategic planning, and optimize financial resources. These activities include budgeting and forecasting, financial reporting, cost management, financial analysis, financial modeling, risk management, treasury management, and compliance.

This book will provide a comprehensive overview of FinOps, covering the key topics and activities essential for managing financial operations effectively. Each chapter will delve into a different aspect of FinOps, discussing the tools, techniques, and best practices used by professionals in the field. We will also examine the challenges and pitfalls faced by FinOps professionals and offer strategies for overcoming these challenges.

Whether you are new to FinOps or an experienced professional looking to expand your knowledge, this book is an invaluable resource for building a solid foundation in financial operations' key concepts and skills. By the end of this book, you will have a thorough understanding of the role FinOps plays in driving organizational success and how you can excel in this field. So let's get started on this journey into the world of FinOps!

CHAPTER 1
BUDGETING AND FORECASTING IN FINOPS
ESSENTIAL TOOLS FOR PLANNING AND MANAGING FINANCIAL RESOURCES

n this chapter, we will explore the role of budgeting and forecasting in FinOps and how you can use these tools to plan for the financial needs of an organization. We will examine the different types of budgets, including operational, capital, and cash, and the key components of a budget, such as revenue and expenses. We will also discuss the importance of forecasting in FinOps, including financial modeling and scenario analysis techniques, and how you can use forecasts to make informed decisions about resource allocation.

We will also cover best practices for developing and implementing budgets and forecasts, including the importance of collaboration and communication with key stakeholders. Finally, we will discuss common challenges and pitfalls to avoid when working with budgeting and forecasting in FinOps.

Budgeting and forecasting are essential tools in FinOps for planning and managing an organization's financial resources. Budgeting involves setting financial targets and allocating resources to achieve those targets. In contrast, forecasting involves making predictions about future financial performance based on past trends and other relevant data.

FinOps professionals may work with several types of budgets, including operational, capital, and cash. Operational budgets focus on an organization's day-to-day expenses, such as salaries, utilities, and rent. On the other hand, capital budgets focus on long-term investments, such as purchasing new equipment or expanding into a new market. Finally, cash budgets track the inflow and outflow of cash within an organization, helping to ensure that there are sufficient funds available to meet financial obligations.

Budgets typically consist of several key components, including revenue, expenses, and capital expenditures. Revenue refers to the income generated by an organization, such as sales, fees, and grants. Expenses refer to the costs associated with running the organization, including operational costs, such as salaries and rent, and capital costs, such as purchasing new equipment. Finally, capital expenditures refer to large, long-term investments in the organization, such as expansion into a new market or building a new facility.

Forecasting is an important part of FinOps, as it helps organizations to make informed decisions about resource allocation and financial strategy. There are several techniques that FinOps professionals may use to make forecasts, including financial modeling and scenario analysis.

Financial modeling involves building a mathematical representation of an organization's financial performance based on various assumptions and inputs. Scenario analysis involves simulating different potential outcomes based on assumptions and variables, such as changes in market conditions or shifts in consumer demand.

Developing and implementing budgets and forecasts involves

collaboration and communication with key stakeholders, such as upper management, financial analysts, and operational teams. Therefore, it is important to involve all relevant parties in the budgeting and forecasting process to ensure that all necessary information is considered and that there is buy-in from all stakeholders.

There are several challenges and pitfalls to avoid when budgeting and forecasting in FinOps. One common challenge is the **difficulty in accurately predicting future financial performance**, which can impact various factors, such as market conditions, consumer demand, and external economic events. It is important to be aware of these uncertainties and use various forecasting techniques to mitigate potential risks.

Another challenge is balancing short-term and long-term financial goals and the competing priorities of different stakeholders. It is important to find a balance between long-term investments and short-term needs and to communicate effectively with all stakeholders to ensure that budgets and forecasts align with overall organizational goals.

In conclusion, budgeting and forecasting are important tools in FinOps for planning and managing an organization's financial resources. Budgeting involves setting financial targets and allocating resources to achieve those targets. In contrast, forecasting involves making predictions about future financial performance. FinOps professionals may work with several types of budgets, including operational, capital, and cash budgets, typically consisting of key components such as revenue, expenses, and capital expenditures.

Forecasting involves financial modeling and scenario analysis techniques to make informed decisions about resource allocation and financial strategy. Developing and implementing budgets and forecasts involves collaboration and communication with key stakeholders. Knowing the challenges and pitfalls that can arise when working with these tools is important. Budgeting and forecasting are essential for ensuring that an organization's financial resources are used effectively and efficiently to support its goals and objectives.

CHAPTER SUMMARY

- Budgeting and forecasting are essential tools in FinOps for planning and managing financial resources.
- There are different types of budgets in FinOps, including operational, capital, and cash.
- Key components of a budget include revenue, expenses, and capital expenditures.
- Forecasting involves predicting future financial performance using financial modeling and scenario analysis techniques.
- Developing and implementing budgets and forecasts requires collaboration and communication with key stakeholders.
- Common challenges in budgeting and forecasting include accurately predicting future financial performance and balancing short-term and long-term financial goals.
- Best practices for budgeting and forecasting include regularly reviewing and updating budgets and forecasts, being transparent about assumptions and limitations, and being flexible and adaptable to change.
- Pitfalls to avoid in budgeting and forecasting include relying on incomplete or outdated data, being overly optimistic or pessimistic, and failing to consider the impact of external factors.

CHAPTER 2
FINANCIAL REPORTING IN FINOPS
UNDERSTANDING AND ANALYZING KEY FINANCIAL DOCUMENTS

n this chapter, we will explore the role of financial reporting in FinOps and how FinOps professionals use financial reports to understand and analyze the financial health of an organization. First, we will examine the different types of financial reports, including income statements, balance sheets, and cash flow statements, and the key components of each report. We will also discuss the importance of financial ratios, such as the debt-to-equity ratio and the return on investment, and how these ratios can be used to evaluate an organization's financial performance.

Next, we will cover best practices for generating and analyzing financial reports, including the importance of accuracy and transparency. Next, we will discuss common challenges and pitfalls to avoid when working with financial reporting in FinOps. Finally, we will discuss the role of financial reporting in decision-making and how financial reports can be used to inform strategic planning and resource allocation.

Financial reporting is an essential component of FinOps. It involves generating and analyzing financial documents to provide a snapshot of an organization's financial health. **FinOps profes-**

sionals are responsible for creating and reviewing financial reports to understand an organization's financial performance and identify areas for improvement. Examples include income statements, balance sheets, and cash flow statements.

One of the key financial reports in FinOps is the income statement, which presents a summary of an organization's revenues and expenses over a specific period, such as a month or a year. The income statement includes key components such as gross, net, and net income. It provides a snapshot of an organization's profitability.

Another important financial report is the balance sheet, which presents a snapshot of an organization's assets, liabilities, and equity at a specific time. The balance sheet is divided into two main sections: the **assets section**, which lists the organization's assets in liquidity, and the **liabilities and equity section**, which lists the organization's liabilities and equity in order of maturity. The balance sheet provides valuable information about an organization's financial position, including its level of debt and the strength of its equity.

The cash flow statement is another key financial report that provides information about the inflow and outflow of cash within an organization. The cash flow statement is divided into three main sections:

- Cash flow from **operating activities**
- Cash flow from **investing activities**
- Cash flow from **financing activities**

The cash flow statement provides valuable insights into an organization's liquidity and financial stability, showing how the organization generates and uses cash.

Financial ratios are another important tool in FinOps for evaluating an organization's financial performance. Financial ratios are calculated by dividing one financial measure by another, providing a way to compare different aspects of an organization's financial performance. Some common financial ratios used in FinOps include the debt-to-equity ratio, which measures an organization's level of debt relative to its equity, and the return on investment (ROI), which measures the profitability of an organization's investments.

Generating and analyzing financial reports involves several best practices, including accuracy and transparency. It is important to ensure that financial reports are accurate and reliable, as they provide a crucial foundation for decision-making and strategic planning. Financial reports should also be transparent. You should easily understand them and make them accessible to all relevant stakeholders.

There are several challenges and pitfalls to avoid when working with financial reporting in FinOps. One common challenge is balancing the need for accuracy and transparency with the need for confidentiality. Financial reports often contain sensitive information. It is important to ensure that this information is protected while still being accessible to those who need it.

Another challenge is keeping financial reports up-to-date, as financial conditions can change rapidly. It is important to regularly review and update financial reports to reflect the organization's current financial situation.

Overall, financial reporting is an essential component of FinOps, as it provides valuable insights into the financial health of an organization and helps inform decision-making and strategic planning. By understanding and analyzing key financial documents, FinOps professionals can ensure that an organization's financial resources are being used effectively and efficiently to support its goals and objectives.

CHAPTER SUMMARY

- Financial reporting is a key aspect of FinOps, involving creating and analyzing financial documents to understand an organization's financial health.
- There are different financial reports, including income statements, balance sheets, and cash flow statements.
- Financial ratios, such as the debt-to-equity ratio and return on investment, are used to evaluate an organization's financial performance.
- Best practices for generating and analyzing financial reports include accuracy and transparency.
- Challenges in financial reporting include balancing confidentiality and transparency, dealing with incomplete or outdated data, and ensuring compliance with regulations and standards.
- Pitfalls to avoid in financial reporting include failing to consider the context of the financial reports, relying on a single financial ratio, and failing to communicate financial information effectively.
- Financial reporting is important for decision-making and strategic planning, and financial reports can inform resource allocation and identify areas for improvement.
- Financial reporting is an ongoing process. It is important to regularly review and update financial reports to ensure they remain accurate and relevant.

CHAPTER 3
COST MANAGEMENT IN FINOPS
IDENTIFYING AND ELIMINATING WASTE TO INCREASE EFFICIENCY AND PROF TABILITY

n this chapter, we will explore the role of cost management in FinOps and how FinOps professionals work to identify and eliminate unnecessary costs and optimize resource use to increase efficiency and profitability. We will examine the different types of costs that organizations face, including fixed, variable, and sunk costs, and how these can be managed effectively. We will also discuss the cost-benefit analysis and cost-cutting measures and how to use these techniques to identify and eliminate waste and inefficiencies.

We will cover best practices for cost management in FinOps, including the importance of collaboration and communication with key stakeholders. We will also discuss common challenges and pitfalls to avoid when working with cost management in FinOps. Finally, we will discuss the role of cost management in decision-making and how you can use cost management to inform strategic planning and resource allocation.

Cost management is a critical aspect of FinOps. It involves **identifying and eliminating unnecessary costs and optimizing resource use to increase efficiency and profitability**. FinOps professionals work to understand the different types of costs that organizations face and how they can manage these costs effectively.

There are several types of costs that organizations may encounter, including fixed costs, variable costs, and sunk costs. Fixed costs are expenses that do not change with changes in output, such as rent and salaries. Variable costs are expenses that vary with changes in output, such as raw materials and labor. Finally, sunk costs are expenses that have already been incurred and cannot be recovered, such as the cost of research and development.

Cost-benefit analysis is a technique that FinOps professionals may use to evaluate the costs and benefits of a particular action or decision. This involves calculating the costs of an action or decision and comparing them to the expected benefits. Cost-benefit analysis can help FinOps professionals to identify the most cost-effective course of action and to make informed decisions about resource allocation.

Cost-cutting measures are another important tool in cost management, as they involve identifying and eliminating waste and inefficiencies within an organization. This can involve streamlining processes, reducing unnecessary expenses, and finding more efficient ways of using resources. Cost-cutting measures can be an effective way to increase efficiency and profitability, and they can be implemented at all levels of an organization, from operational processes to strategic planning.

Effective cost management involves collaboration and communication with key stakeholders, including upper management, financial analysts, and operational teams. Therefore, it is important to involve all relevant parties in the cost management process to ensure that all necessary information is considered and that there is buy-in from all stakeholders.

There are several challenges and pitfalls to avoid when working with cost management in FinOps. One common challenge is *balancing short-term and long-term financial goals* and the competing priorities of different stakeholders. It is important to balance reducing costs, investing in long-term growth, and communicating effectively with all stakeholders to ensure that cost management efforts align with overall organizaticnal goals.

Another challenge is the need to accurately predict the impact of cost-cutting measures, as it can be difficult to predict the full consequences of a particular action or decision. Therefore, it is important to carefully consider any cost-cutting measure's potential risks and benefits and implement these measures to minimize disruption and maximize the desired outcomes.

Overall, cost management is an essential component of FinOps, as it helps organizations identify and eliminate waste and inefficiencies and optimize the use of resources to increase efficiency and profitability. By understanding and managing costs effectively, FinOps professionals can ensure that an organization's financial resources are being used effectively and efficiently to support its goals and objectives.

CHAPTER SUMMARY

- Cost management is a key aspect of FinOps, involving identifying and eliminating unnecessary costs and optimizing resource use to increase efficiency and profitability.
- Organizations face different costs, including fixed, variable, and sunk costs.
- Cost-benefit analysis and cost-cutting measures are techniques used in cost management to identify and eliminate waste and inefficiencies.
- Effective cost management involves collaboration and communication with key stakeholders.
- Challenges in cost management include balancing short-term and long-term financial goals and accurately predicting the impact of cost-cutting measures.
- Pitfalls to avoid in cost management include failing to consider the full consequences of a cost-cutting measure and failing to communicate effectively with stakeholders.
- Cost management is important for decision-making and strategic planning, and you can use it to inform resource allocation and identify areas for improvement.
- Regular review and update of cost management strategies are important to ensure they remain effective and relevant.

CHAPTER 4
FINANCIAL ANALYSIS IN FINOPS
EVALUATING AND IMPROVING FINANCIAL PERFORMANCE THROUGH RATIO ANALYSIS AND TREND ANALYSIS

n this chapter, we will explore the role of financial analysis in FinOps and how FinOps professionals use financial analysis techniques to evaluate an organization's financial performance and identify areas for improvement. We will examine the different types of financial analysis techniques, including ratio and trend analysis, and how you can use these techniques to understand an organization's financial performance. We will also discuss the importance of financial ratios, such as the debt-to-equity ratio and the return on investment, and how these ratios can be used to evaluate an organization's financial performance.

We will cover best practices for financial analysis in FinOps, including the importance of using accurate and up-to-date data, and we will discuss common challenges and pitfalls to avoid when working with financial analysis in FinOps. Finally, we will discuss the role of financial analysis in decision-making and how financial analysis can inform strategic planning and resource allocation.

Financial analysis is an essential component of FinOps, as it involves evaluating an organization's financial performance and identifying areas for improvement. FinOps professionals use various financial analysis techniques to understand an organization's financial performance, including ratio and trend analysis.

Ratio analysis is a technique that involves comparing different financial measures to understand the financial performance of an organization. Financial ratios are calculated by dividing one financial measure by another, providing a way to compare different aspects of an organization's financial performance. Some common financial ratios used in FinOps include the **debt-to-equity ratio,** which measures an organization's level of debt relative to its equity, and the **return on investment** (ROI), which measures the profitability of an organization's investments.

Trend analysis is another technique that FinOps professionals may use to understand an organization's financial performance. This involves analyzing financial data over time, such as several months or years, to identify trends and patterns in the data. Trend analysis can identify areas of strength and weakness in an organization's financial performance and identify potential improvement opportunities.

Effective financial analysis in FinOps involves using accurate and up-to-date data and applying appropriate financial analysis techniques to the data. It is also important to consider the context in which the data is being analyzed, as external factors such as market conditions and industry trends can impact an organization's financial performance.

There are several challenges and pitfalls to avoid when working with financial analysis in FinOps. One common challenge is the need to ensure the accuracy and reliability of the data being analyzed. Financial data can be complex and can be impacted by various factors. Therefore, ensuring that the data used is accurate and complete is important.

Another challenge is keeping financial data up-to-date, as financial conditions can change rapidly. Therefore, it is important to regularly review and update financial data to reflect the organization's current financial situation.

Financial analysis is an essential component of FinOps, as it helps organizations understand and improve their financial performance. FinOps professionals can identify areas for improvement and make informed decisions about resource allocation and financial strategy using financial analysis techniques such as ratio analysis and trend analysis.

CHAPTER SUMMARY

- Financial analysis is a key aspect of FinOps, involving evaluating an organization's financial performance and identifying areas for improvement.
- Financial analysis techniques include ratio analysis and trend analysis.
- Financial ratios, such as the debt-to-equity ratio and return on investment, are used to evaluate an organization's financial performance.
- Effective financial analysis requires accurate and up-to-date data and consideration of the context in which the data is being analyzed.
- Challenges in the financial analysis include ensuring the accuracy and reliability of the data and keeping financial data up-to-date.
- Pitfalls to avoid in the financial analysis include failing to consider the context of the data and relying on a single financial ratio.
- Financial analysis is important for decision-making and strategic planning, and it can inform resource allocation and identify areas for improvement.
- Regular review and update of financial data are important to ensure that it reflects the organization's current financial situation.

CHAPTER 5
FINANCIAL MODELING IN FINOPS
SIMULATING DIFFERENT SCENARIOS TO INFORM FUTURE FINANCIAL STRATEGIES

n this chapter, we will explore the role of financial modeling in FinOps and how FinOps professionals use financial models to simulate different scenarios and make informed decisions about future financial strategies. We will examine the different types of financial models, including static and dynamic models, and how these models can be used to understand the financial impacts of different actions or decisions. We will also discuss the importance of assumptions in financial modeling and how to choose appropriate assumptions to ensure the accuracy and reliability of financial models.

We will cover best practices for financial modeling in FinOps, including the importance of collaboration and communication with key stakeholders. We will also discuss common challenges and pitfalls to avoid when working with financial modeling in FinOps. Finally, we will discuss the role of financial modeling in decision-making and how financial modeling can be used to inform strategic planning and resource allocation.

Financial modeling is a key tool in FinOps for simulating different scenarios and making informed decisions about future financial strategies. Financial models are *mathematical representations* of an organization's financial performance based on various assumptions and inputs. FinOps professionals use financial models to understand the financial impacts of different actions or decisions and to make informed decisions about resource allocation and financial strategy.

There are two main types of financial models: **static models** and **dynamic models**. Static models are designed to analyze a single scenario, such as the financial impacts of a particular action or decision. On the other hand, dynamic models are designed to analyze multiple scenarios and understand how an organization's financial performance may change over time based on different assumptions and inputs.

Assumptions are an important component of financial modeling, as they provide the foundation for the model and help to ensure its accuracy and reliability. Therefore, choosing appropriate assumptions for a financial model is important based on the specific context in which you will use it. For example, assumptions about market conditions, consumer demand, and external economic factors can all impact the accuracy of a financial model.

Effective financial modeling in FinOps involves collaboration and communication with key stakeholders, including upper management, financial analysts, and operational teams. Therefore, it is important to involve all relevant parties in the financial modeling process to ensure that all necessary information is considered and that there is buy-in from all stakeholders.

There are several challenges and pitfalls to avoid when working with financial modeling in FinOps. One common challenge is accurately predicting future financial performance, which various factors, such as market conditions, consumer demand, and external economic events, can impact. Therefore, it is important to be aware of these uncertainties and use various forecasting techniques to mitigate potential risks.

Another challenge is balancing the need for accuracy and reliability with the flexibility, as **financial models may need to be revised as new information becomes available**. Therefore, it is important to regularly review and update financial models to ensure that they reflect the organization's current financial situation.

In conclusion, financial modeling is a powerful tool in FinOps for simulating different scenarios and making informed decisions about future financial strategies. Financial models are mathematical representations of an organization's financial performance based on various assumptions and inputs. You can use them to understand the financial impacts of different actions or decisions. There are two main types of financial models: static models and dynamic models. It is important to choose appropriate assumptions to ensure the accuracy and reliability of financial models.

Effective financial modeling involves collaboration and communication with key stakeholders. It is important to be aware of the challenges and pitfalls that can arise when working with financial models, such as the difficulty in accurately predicting future financial performance and the need to balance accuracy and flexibility. Financial modeling is an essential tool in FinOps for informing decision-making and strategic planning. It can help organizations optimize their financial resources to achieve their goals and objectives.

CHAPTER SUMMARY

- Financial modeling is a tool used in FinOps to simulate different scenarios and inform future financial strategies.
- There are two main types of financial models: static models and dynamic models.
- Assumptions are an important component of financial modeling, and choosing appropriate assumptions is crucial to ensure accuracy and reliability.
- Effective financial modeling in FinOps involves collaboration and communication with key stakeholders.
- Challenges in financial modeling include accurately predicting future financial performance and balancing accuracy and flexibility.
- Financial modeling can inform decision-making and help with strategic planning and resource allocation.
- Best practices for financial modeling include using accurate and up-to-date data, regularly reviewing and updating models, and considering the context in which the model will be used.
- Pitfalls to avoid in financial modeling include relying on incomplete or outdated data and making unrealistic assumptions.

CHAPTER 6
RISK MANAGEMENT IN FINOPS
PROTECTING FINANCIAL ASSETS THROUGH INSURANCE AND HEDGING

n this chapter, we will explore the role of risk management in FinOps and how FinOps professionals use risk management techniques, such as insurance and hedging, to protect an organization's financial assets from potential risks. We will examine the different types of risks that organizations may face, including financial, operational, and reputational risks, and how you can manage these risks effectively. We will also discuss the importance of risk assessment and risk management planning and how you can use these techniques to identify and prioritize risks.

We will cover best practices for risk management in FinOps, including the importance of collaboration and communication with key stakeholders. We will also discuss common challenges and pitfalls to avoid when working with risk management in FinOps. Finally, we will discuss the role of risk management in decision-making and how you can use risk management to inform strategic planning and resource allocation.

Risk management is critical to FinOps, protecting an organization's financial assets from potential risks. FinOps professionals use a range of risk management techniques, such as **insurance** and

hedging, to mitigate potential risks and ensure the stability and security of an organization's financial assets.

There are several types of risks that organizations may face, including financial risks, operational risks, and reputational risks. Financial risks may impact an organization's financial performance, such as market risks, credit risks, and liquidity risks. Operational risks such as supply chain disruptions and regulatory and technological risks may impact an organization's operations. Finally, reputational risks such as negative publicity, data breaches, and customer dissatisfaction may impact an organization's reputation.

Risk assessment and risk management planning are important techniques in risk management, as they help to identify and prioritize risks. Risk assessment involves identifying and evaluating potential risks. In contrast, risk management planning involves developing strategies to mitigate or eliminate these risks. Therefore, it is important to regularly review and update risk assessment and management plans to ensure that they reflect the current risk profile of the organization.

Effective risk management in FinOps involves collaboration and communication with key stakeholders, including upper management, financial analysts, and operational teams. Therefore, it is important to involve all relevant parties in the risk management process to ensure that all necessary information is considered and that there is buy-in from all stakeholders.

In conclusion, risk management is an essential component of FinOps. It helps organizations protect their financial assets from potential risks. FinOps professionals use a range of risk management techniques, such as insurance and hedging, to mitigate potential risks and ensure the stability and security of an organization's financial assets. Risk assessment and risk management planning are important techniques in risk management, as they help identify and prioritize risks and develop strategies to mitigate or eliminate them.

Effective risk management involves collaboration and communication with key stakeholders. It is important to be aware of the challenges and pitfalls that can arise when working with risk management, such as the need to predict future risks accurately and balance risk and reward. Overall, risk management is an essential component of FinOps for informing decision-making and strategic planning. It can help organizations optimize their financial resources to achieve their goals and objectives.

CHAPTER SUMMARY

- Risk management is an essential component of FinOps, as it helps to protect an organization's financial assets from potential risks.
- There are several types of risks that organizations may face, including financial risks, operational risks, and reputational risks.
- Risk assessment and risk management planning are important techniques in risk management, as they help to identify and prioritize risks.
- Risk management techniques used in FinOps include insurance and hedging.
- Effective risk management involves collaboration and communication with key stakeholders.
- Risk management challenges include accurately predicting future risks and balancing risk and reward.
- Risk management is important for decision-making and strategic planning in FinOps, as it helps organizations optimize their financial resources to achieve their goals and objectives.
- Pitfalls to avoid in risk management include failing to consider all relevant information and not involving all relevant stakeholders in the risk management process.

CHAPTER 7
TREASURY MANAGEMENT IN FINOPS
MANAGING CASH FLOW, DEBT, AND SURPLUS FUNDS

n this chapter, we will explore the role of treasury management in FinOps and how FinOps professionals manage an organization's cash flow, including forecasting cash needs, managing debt, and investing surplus funds. We will examine the aspects of treasury management, including cash management, debt management, and investment management, and how you can coordinate these activities effectively. We will also discuss the importance of forecasting cash needs and managing liquidity and how you can use these techniques to ensure that an organization has sufficient cash to meet its financial obligations.

We will cover best practices for treasury management in FinOps, including the importance of collaboration and communication with key stakeholders. We will also discuss common challenges and pitfalls to avoid when working with treasury management in FinOps. Finally, we will discuss the role of treasury management in decision-making and how you can use treasury management to inform strategic planning and resource allocation.

Treasury management is a critical aspect of FinOps. It involves managing an organization's cash flow, forecasting cash needs, managing debt, and investing surplus funds. FinOps professionals coordinate these activities to ensure that an organization's financial resources are used effectively and efficiently.

FinOps professionals may be responsible for several aspects of treasury management, including **cash management, debt management**, and **investment management**. Cash management involves forecasting cash needs and managing liquidity to ensure that an organization has sufficient cash to meet its financial obligations. Debt management involves managing an organization's debt portfolio, including negotiating loan terms and managing debt repayment. Finally, investment management involves investing surplus funds to maximize returns and minimize risk.

Effective treasury management in FinOps involves collaboration and communication with key stakeholders, including upper management, financial analysts, and operational teams. Therefore, it is important to involve all relevant parties in the treasury management process to ensure that all necessary information is considered and that there is buy-in from all stakeholders.

There are several challenges and pitfalls to avoid when working with treasury management in FinOps. One common challenge is accurately predicting cash needs and managing liquidity. Financial conditions can change rapidly, and unexpected events can impact cash flow. Therefore, it is important to regularly review and update cash flow forecasts and have contingency plans to manage unexpected cash flow changes.

Another challenge is balancing short-term and long-term financial goals and the competing priorities of different stakeholders. It is important to balance maximizing short-term returns, investing in long-term growth, and communicating effectively with all stakeholders to ensure that treasury management efforts align with overall organizational goals.

Overall, treasury management is an essential component of FinOps. It helps organizations manage their cash flow effectively and make informed resource allocation and financial strategy decisions. By coordinating the various aspects of treasury management, FinOps professionals can ensure that an organization's financial resources are being used effectively and efficiently to achieve its goals and objectives. Treasury management is also an important component of decision-making in FinOps, as it helps to inform strategic planning and resource allocation by clearly understanding an organization's financial position and future cash flow needs.

CHAPTER SUMMARY

- Treasury management in FinOps involves managing cash flow, forecasting cash needs, managing debt, and investing surplus funds.
- FinOps professionals may be responsible for cash management, debt, and investment management.
- Collaboration and communication with stakeholders and regularly reviewing and updating cash flow forecasts and contingency plans are important in effective treasury management.
- Challenges in treasury management include accurately predicting cash needs, managing liquidity, and balancing short-term and long-term financial goals.
- Treasury management helps organizations make informed resource allocation and financial strategy decisions and ensures that financial resources are used effectively.
- Treasury management informs strategic planning and resource allocation by understanding an organization's financial position and future cash flow needs.
- FinOps professionals can coordinate various aspects of treasury management to optimize financial resources and achieve organizational goals.

CHAPTER 8
COMPLIANCE IN FINOPS
ENSURING ADHERENCE TO FINANCIAL REGULATIONS AND LAWS

n this chapter, we will explore the role of compliance in FinOps and how FinOps professionals ensure that an organization complies with relevant financial regulations and laws, including tax laws, accounting standards, and anti-money laundering regulations. We will examine the different types of financial regulations and laws organizations may need to comply with and how these regulations and laws can impact an organization's financial operations. We will also discuss the importance of developing and implementing effective compliance processes, including risk assessment and monitoring, and how these processes can help ensure that an organization complies with relevant regulations and laws.

We will cover best practices for compliance in FinOps, including the importance of collaboration and communication with key stakeholders. We will also discuss common challenges and pitfalls to avoid when working with compliance in FinOps. Finally, we will discuss the role of compliance in decision-making and how you can use compliance to inform strategic planning and resource allocation.

Compliance is essential to FinOps, ensuring that an organization complies with relevant financial regulations and laws. For example, FinOps professionals ensure that an organization complies with tax laws, accounting standards, and anti-money laundering regulations.

Organizations may need to comply with a wide range of financial regulations and laws, depending on the industry in which they operate and the geographical location in which they do business. These regulations and laws can impact an organization's financial operations in a variety of ways, including the reporting and disclosure of financial information, the management of financial risks, and the handling of financial transactions.

Effective compliance in FinOps involves developing and implementing **effective compliance processes, including risk assessment and monitoring**. Risk assessment involves identifying and evaluating potential compliance risks. In contrast, monitoring involves regularly reviewing and updating compliance processes to ensure that they are effective and that the organization complies with relevant regulations and laws. In addition, it is important to regularly review and update compliance processes to ensure that they reflect the current regulatory environment in which the organization operates.

Effective compliance in FinOps also involves collaboration and communication with key stakeholders, including upper management, financial analysts, and operational teams. Therefore, it is important to involve all relevant parties in the compliance process to ensure that all necessary information is considered and that there is buy-in from all stakeholders.

There are several challenges and pitfalls to avoid when working with compliance in FinOps. One common challenge is keeping up-to-date with regulatory requirements, as financial regulations and laws can change rapidly. It is important to regularly review and update compliance processes to reflect the current regulatory environment.

Another challenge is balancing the need for compliance with operational efficiency, as compliance processes can be time-consuming and resource-intensive. It is important to find a balance between compliance and operational efficiency and to communicate effectively with all stakeholders to ensure compliance efforts align with overall organizational goals.

Overall, compliance is an essential component of FinOps, as it helps organizations comply with relevant financial regulations and laws. By developing and implementing effective compliance processes, FinOps professionals can help organizations minimize the risk of financial penalties and protect the organization's reputation.

Compliance is also an important component of decision-making in FinOps, as it helps to inform strategic planning and resource allocation by clearly understanding the regulatory environment in which the organization operates. Finally, FinOps professionals can help organizations optimize their financial resources to achieve their goals and objectives by ensuring that an organization complies with relevant regulations and laws.

CHAPTER SUMMARY

- Compliance is a crucial aspect of FinOps, ensuring that an organization adheres to financial regulations and laws, including tax and accounting standards.
- Financial regulations and laws can impact an organization's financial operations in various ways, such as reporting and disclosure requirements and managing financial risks.
- Effective compliance in FinOps involves developing and implementing effective compliance processes, including risk assessment and monitoring.
- Compliance processes should be regularly reviewed and updated to reflect the current regulatory environment and identify potential compliance risks.
- Collaboration and communication with key stakeholders are important in compliance, as all relevant parties should be involved in the compliance process.
- Keeping up-to-date with changing regulatory requirements and balancing the need for compliance with operational efficiency are common challenges in compliance.
- Compliance can be an important component of decision-making in FinOps, as it helps inform strategic planning and resource allocation by ensuring that an organization complies with relevant regulations and laws.
- Ensuring compliance is important for minimizing the risk of financial penalties and protecting an organization's reputation.

USING FINOPS TO DRIVE SUCCESS

A CASE STUDY

I n this chapter, we will share a real-life story of how FinOps played a key role in helping a company achieve success. For this chapter, we will use fake names to protect the identity of the individuals and companies involved.

Alice had always been passionate about finance and technology, so when she landed a job as a financial operations specialist at ABC Corporation, she was thrilled. ABC was a mid-sized manufacturing company *struggling to keep up with the rapid pace of change in the industry*. The CFO, Jack, had recently heard about FinOps and saw it as a way to streamline the company's financial operations and increase efficiency. So he brought Alice on board to lead the charge.

At first, Alice faced several challenges while trying to implement FinOps at ABC. Many of the company's financial processes were outdated and inefficient, and there was resistance to change from some finance team members. Alice had to work hard to persuade her colleagues of the benefits of FinOps and to get buy-in from upper management.

One of Alice's first things was to conduct a **financial analysis** to understand the company's current financial performance. She used ratio analysis and trend analysis to identify improvement areas and set financial goals for the company. She then worked with the finance team to implement new financial systems and processes, such as automated invoicing and expense tracking, to help the company meet these goals.

As Alice's efforts began to bear fruit, she encountered another challenge: *the COVID-19 pandemic*. COVID-19 severely impacted ABC's business, and Alice had to pivot quickly to ensure the company's financial stability. She worked closely with the CFO to develop a financial plan to help the company weather the storm. This included finding ways to reduce costs, such as renegotiating vendor contracts and implementing cost-cutting measures, and finding new sources of revenue, such as expanding into new markets.

Despite these challenges, Alice's efforts paid off. ABC's financial performance improved significantly, and the company could weather the pandemic better than many competitors. FinOps became a key part of the company's financial strategy in the years that followed. ABC promoted Alice to FinOps manager.

The success of FinOps at ABC Corporation had a deeper meaning for Alice. It showed her that **finance and technology could work together** to drive positive change in a company and that financial operations specialists had the power to make a real difference in their organizations. It was a lesson she carried with her throughout her career and one that she was proud to pass on to the next generation of FinOps professionals.

In conclusion, FinOps played a crucial role in helping ABC Corporation achieve success. Alice, a financial operations specialist, led the implementation of FinOps at the company, which included conducting financial analysis, implementing new systems and processes, and developing a financial plan in the face of the

COVID-19 pandemic. As a result, ABC's financial performance improved significantly, and the company could weather the pandemic better than many competitors. As a result, FinOps became a key part of the company's financial strategy, and ABC promoted Alice to FinOps manager. The success of FinOps at ABC showed Alice the power of finance and technology working together to drive positive change, and it was a lesson she carried throughout her career.

THE IMPORTANCE OF FINOPS IN FINANCIAL MANAGEMENT AND OPERATIONS

n conclusion, FinOps is a critical function that plays a vital role in organizations' financial management and operations. FinOps professionals are responsible for various activities, including budgeting and forecasting, financial reporting, cost management, financial analysis, financial modeling, risk management, treasury management, and compliance. These activities are interconnected and are crucial in informing decision-making, strategic planning, and optimizing financial resources to achieve organizational goals and objectives.

Effective FinOps requires collaboration and communication with key stakeholders, including upper management, financial analysts, and operational teams. It is important to involve all relevant parties in the FinOps process to ensure that all necessary information is considered and that there is buy-in from all stakeholders.

FinOps also involves navigating various challenges and pitfalls, including accurately predicting future financial performance, balancing short-term and long-term financial goals, and ensuring compliance with relevant regulations and laws. By understanding the various activities and challenges involved in FinOps, organizations can develop and implement effective FinOps strategies to optimize their financial resources and achieve their goals and objectives.

AFTERWORD

As you reach the end of this book, I hope you have gained a deeper understanding of the tools and techniques used in FinOps and feel better equipped to succeed in this exciting field.

FinOps is a dynamic and constantly evolving field. I encourage you to continue learning and staying up-to-date on the latest best practices and developments. As you progress in your career, remember that the key to success in FinOps is being proactive, adaptable, and collaborative.

I also encourage you to take advantage of the many resources available to FinOps professionals, such as professional development courses, networking events, and online communities. These can help you stay connected with your peers, learn from experts in the field, and stay up-to-date on the latest trends and best practices.

I hope this book has been a valuable resource for you. It will continue to be a helpful guide as you advance your career in financial operations. Thank you for reading, and I wish you all the best in your journey.

Sincerely, Peter Bates

ACKNOWLEDGMENTS

Writing a book is a collaborative effort, and I am deeply grateful to all of the individuals and organizations who have contributed to the creation of this book.

First and foremost, I would like to thank my colleagues and peers in FinOps for their invaluable insights, guidance, and support. Your expertise and experience have been essential in shaping the content of this book and ensuring its accuracy and relevance.

I would also like to thank my family and friends for their unwavering support and encouragement throughout this project. Your belief in me and this book has been a constant motivation and inspiration.

Thank you all for your contributions and for making this book a reality.

Sincerely, Peter Bates

ABOUT THE AUTHOR

Peter Bates is a financial operations professional with over ten years of experience. He has a Bachelor's degree in Finance from the University of Chicago. He has worked for several Fortune 500 companies in various roles related to FinOps, including Financial Analyst and Financial Planning and Analysis Manager.

In addition to his professional experience, Peter is passionate about sharing his knowledge and expertise with others. He has taught courses on financial operations at the local community college. He has contributed to industry publications on topics related to budgeting, forecasting, financial analysis, and risk management.

When Peter is not working or writing, he enjoys hiking and traveling with his family. He currently resides in San Francisco with his wife and two children.

www.ingramcontent.com/pod-product-compliance
Lightning Source LLC
Chambersburg PA
CBHW071443210326
41597CB00020B/3926